Too Dark Down There!

Deep Ocean Life Coloring Book

Activibooks for Kids

activibooks for kids

Coloring, Drawing & Activity Books For Children

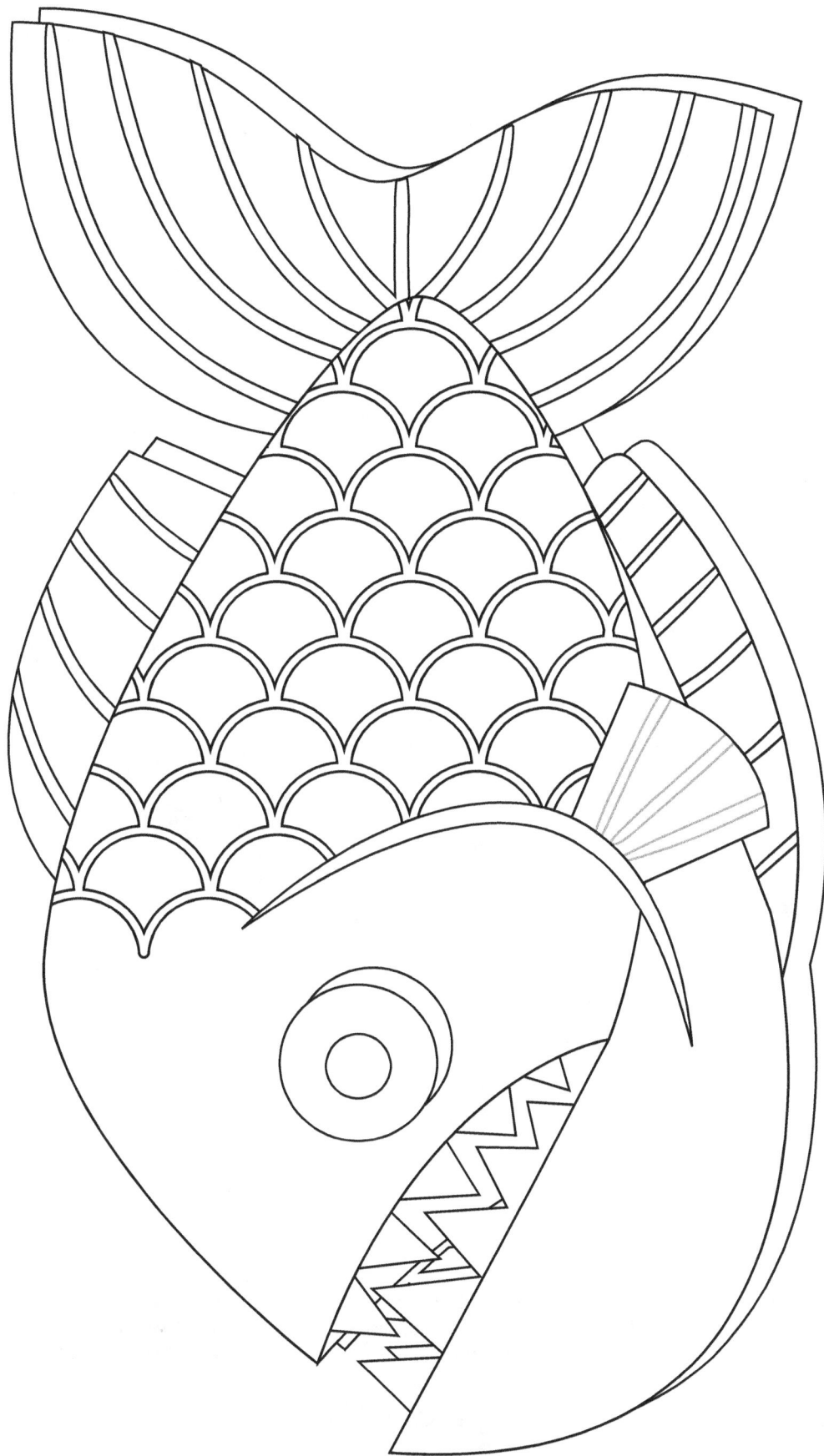

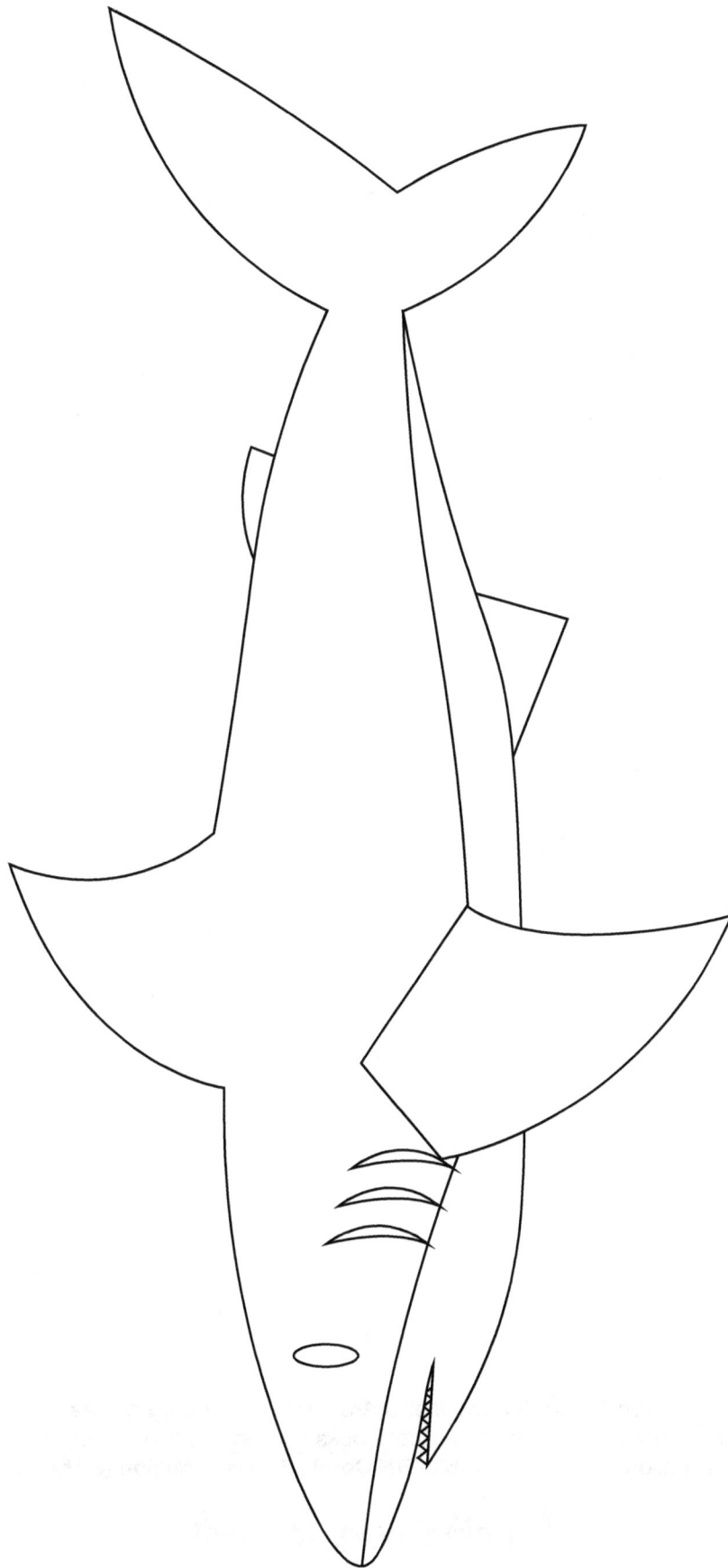

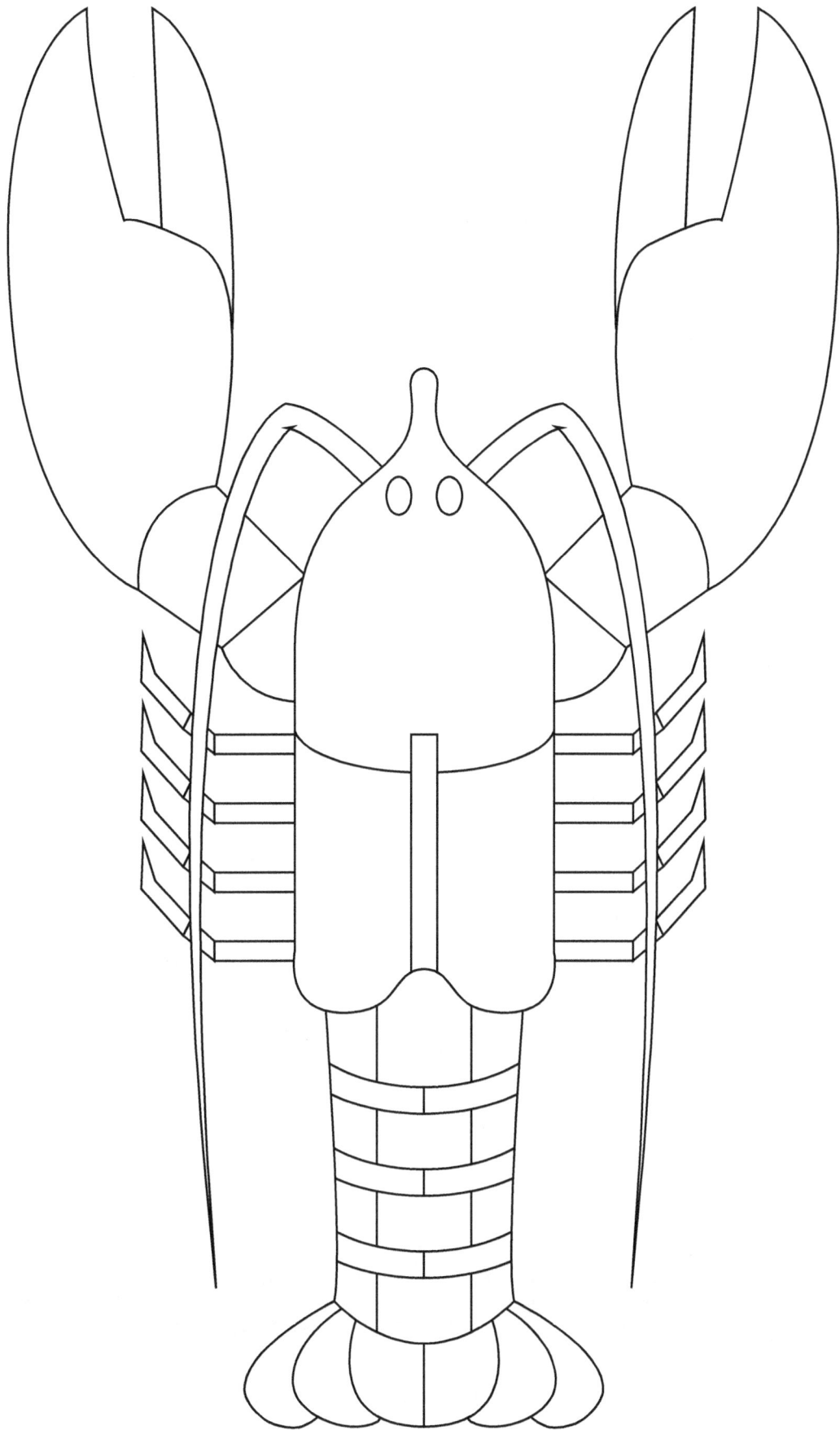

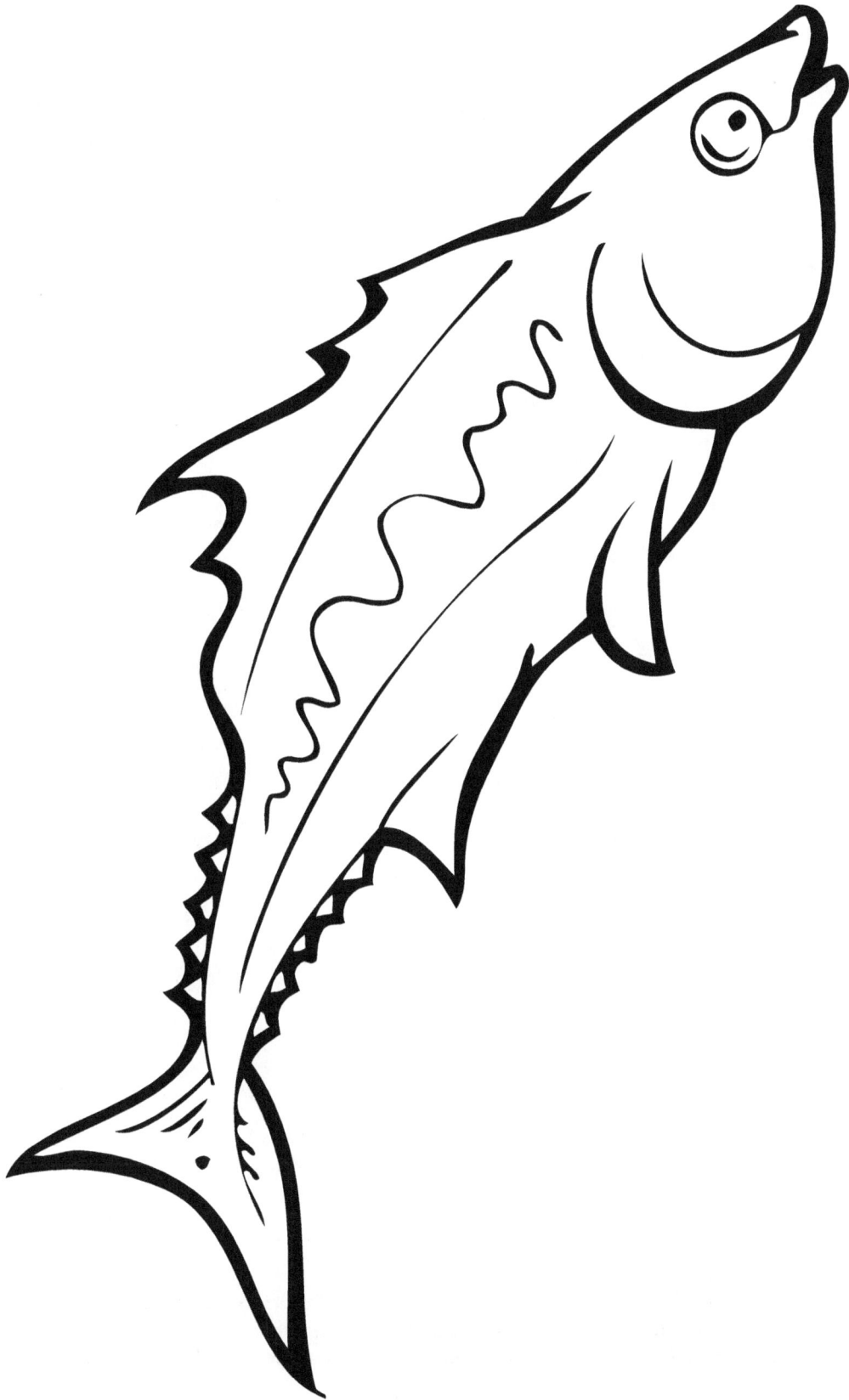

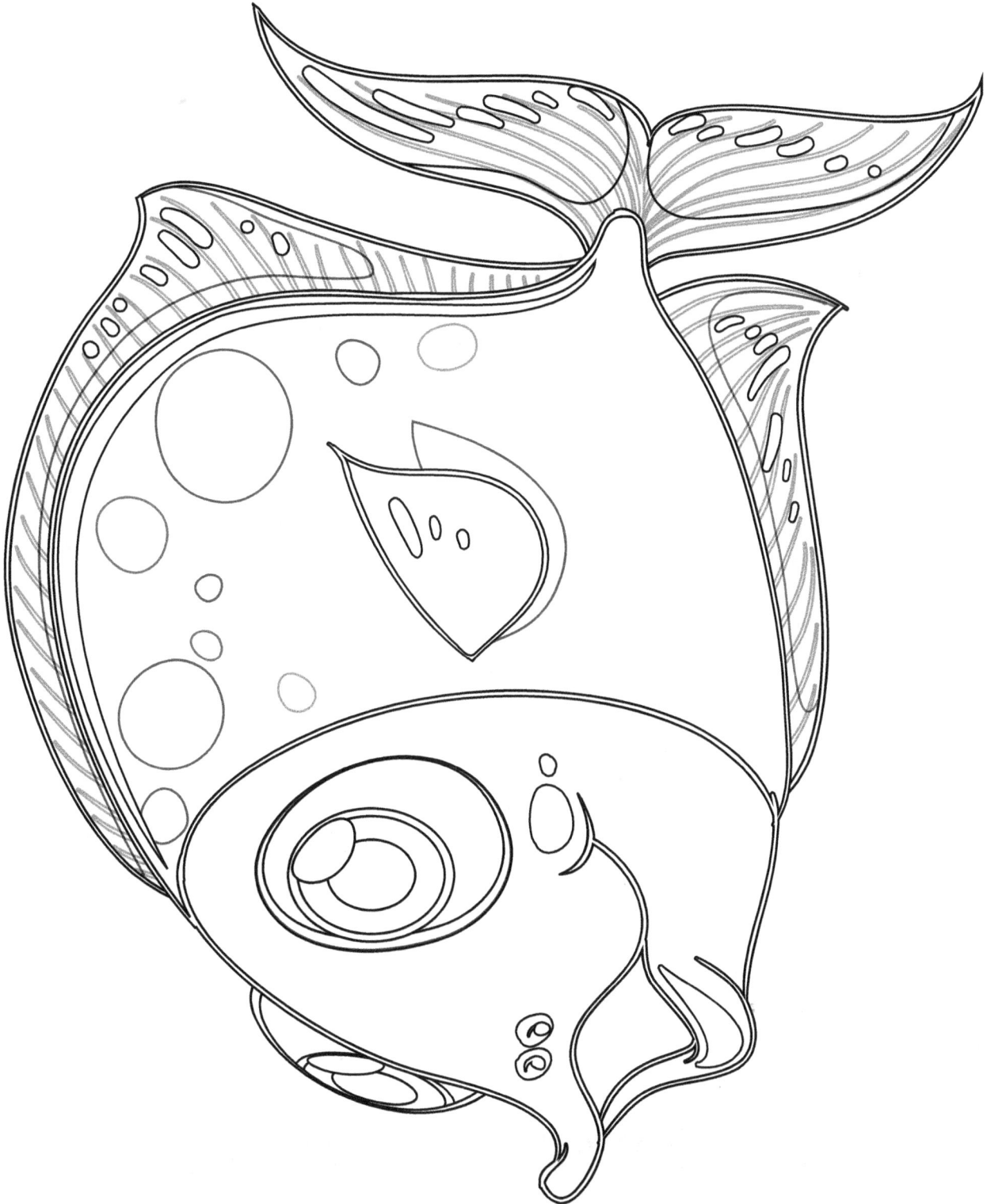

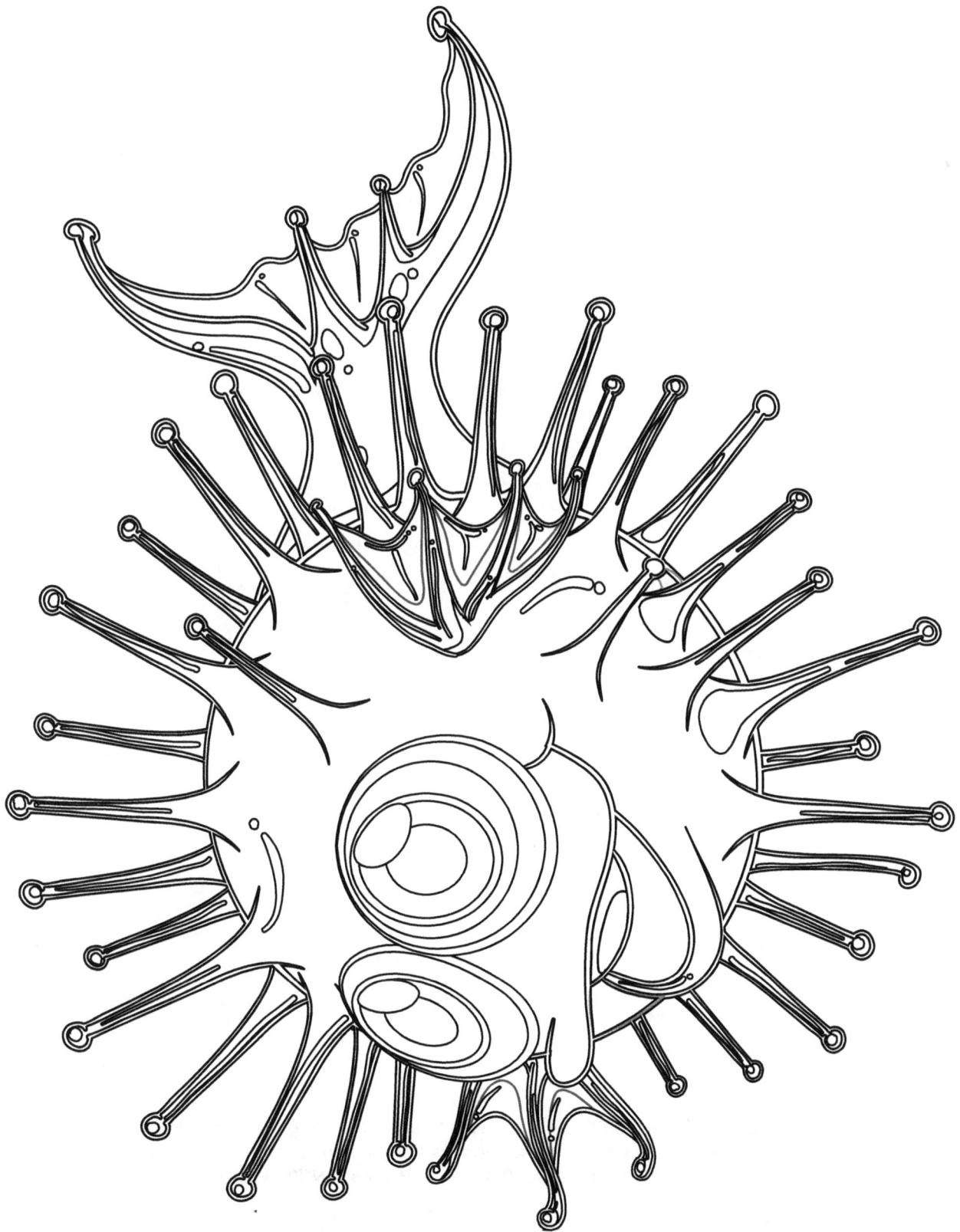

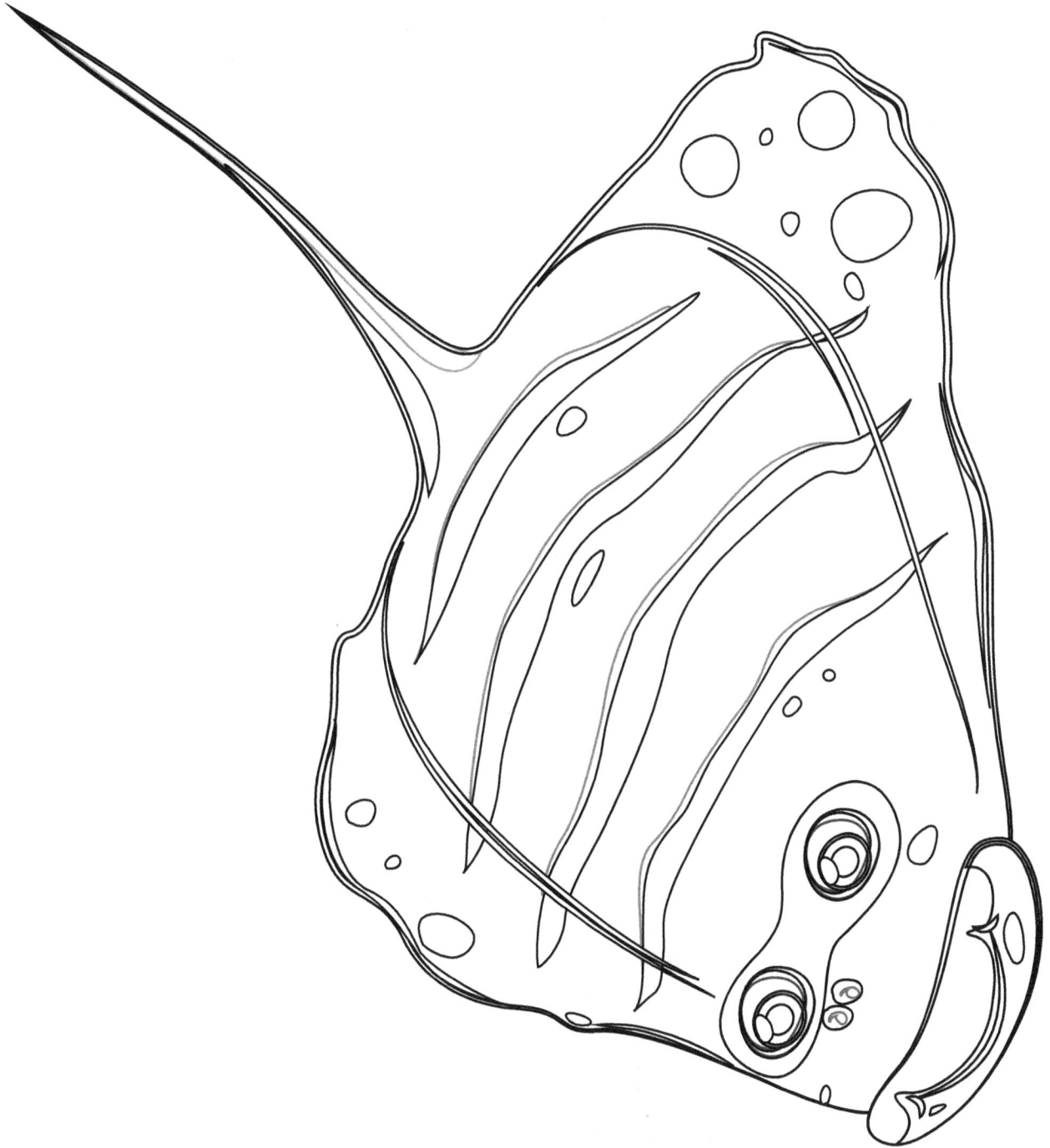

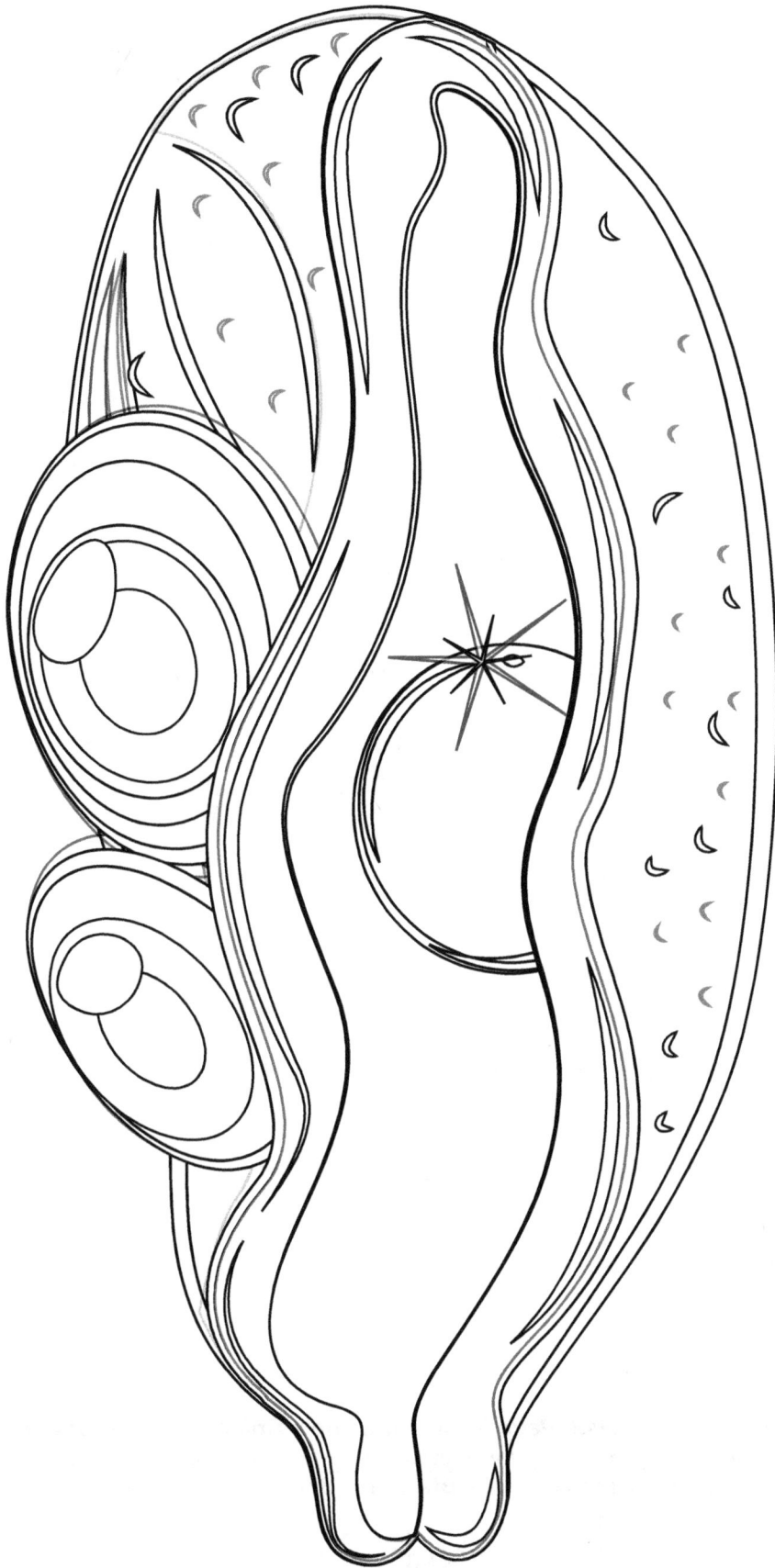

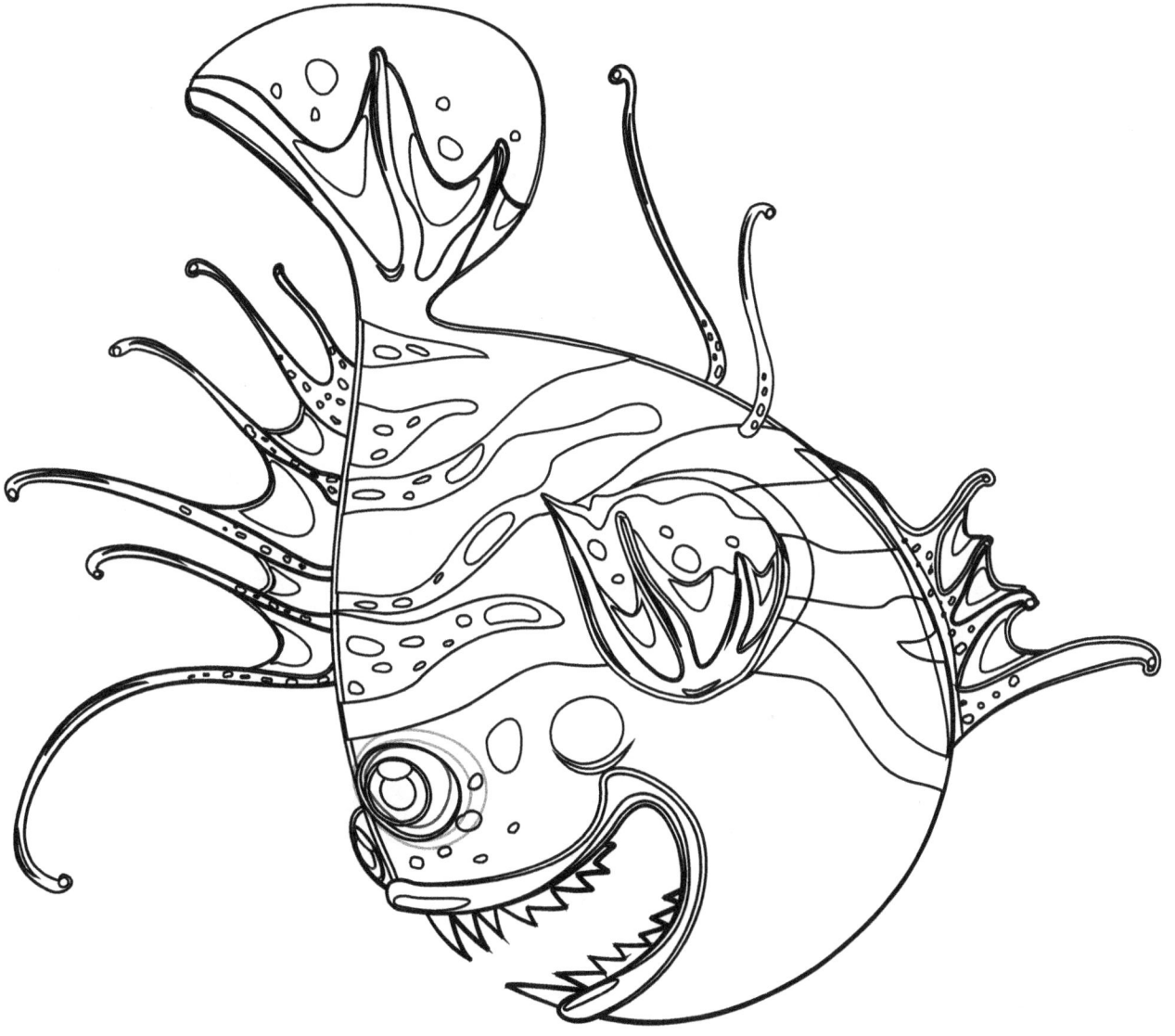

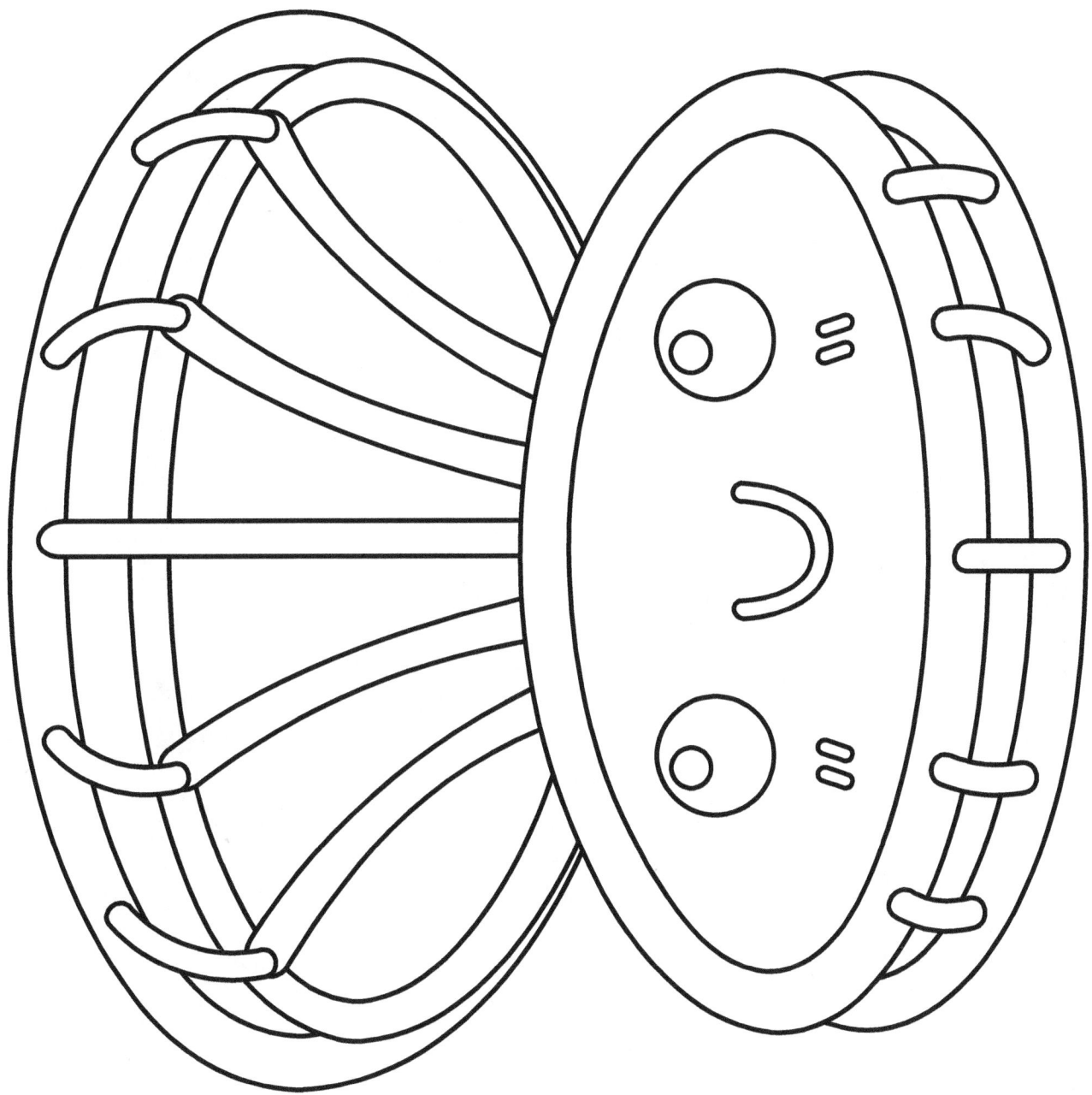

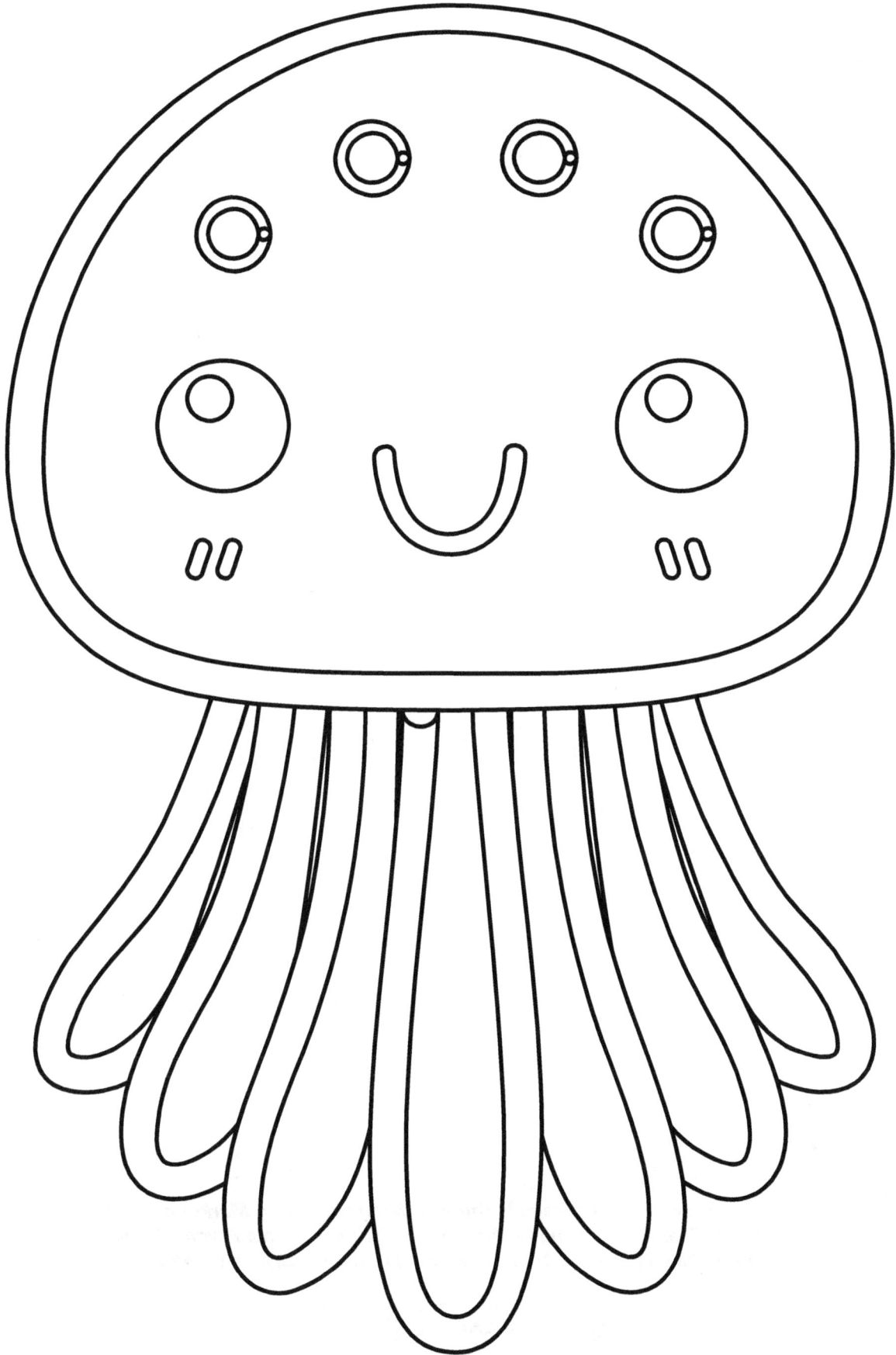

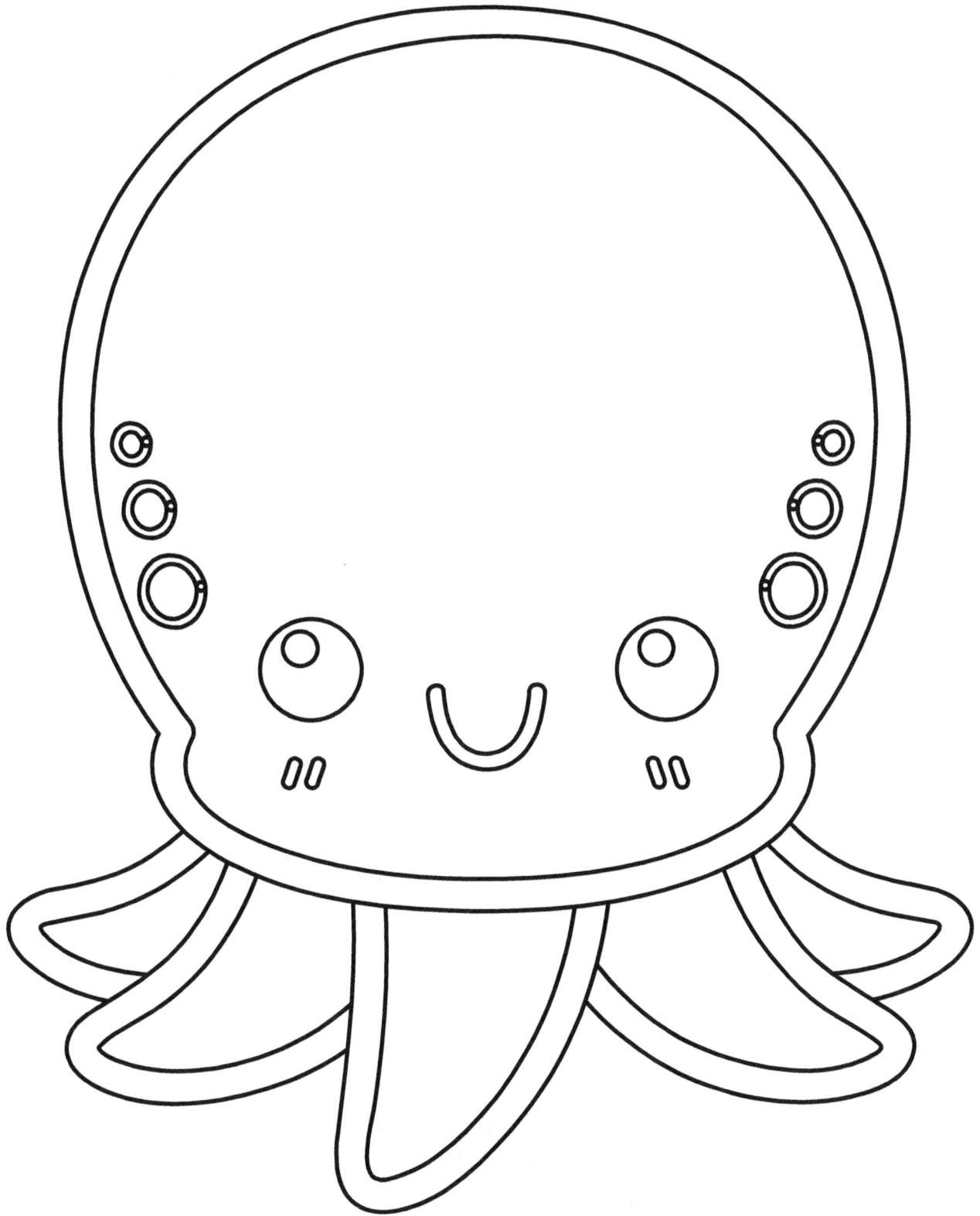

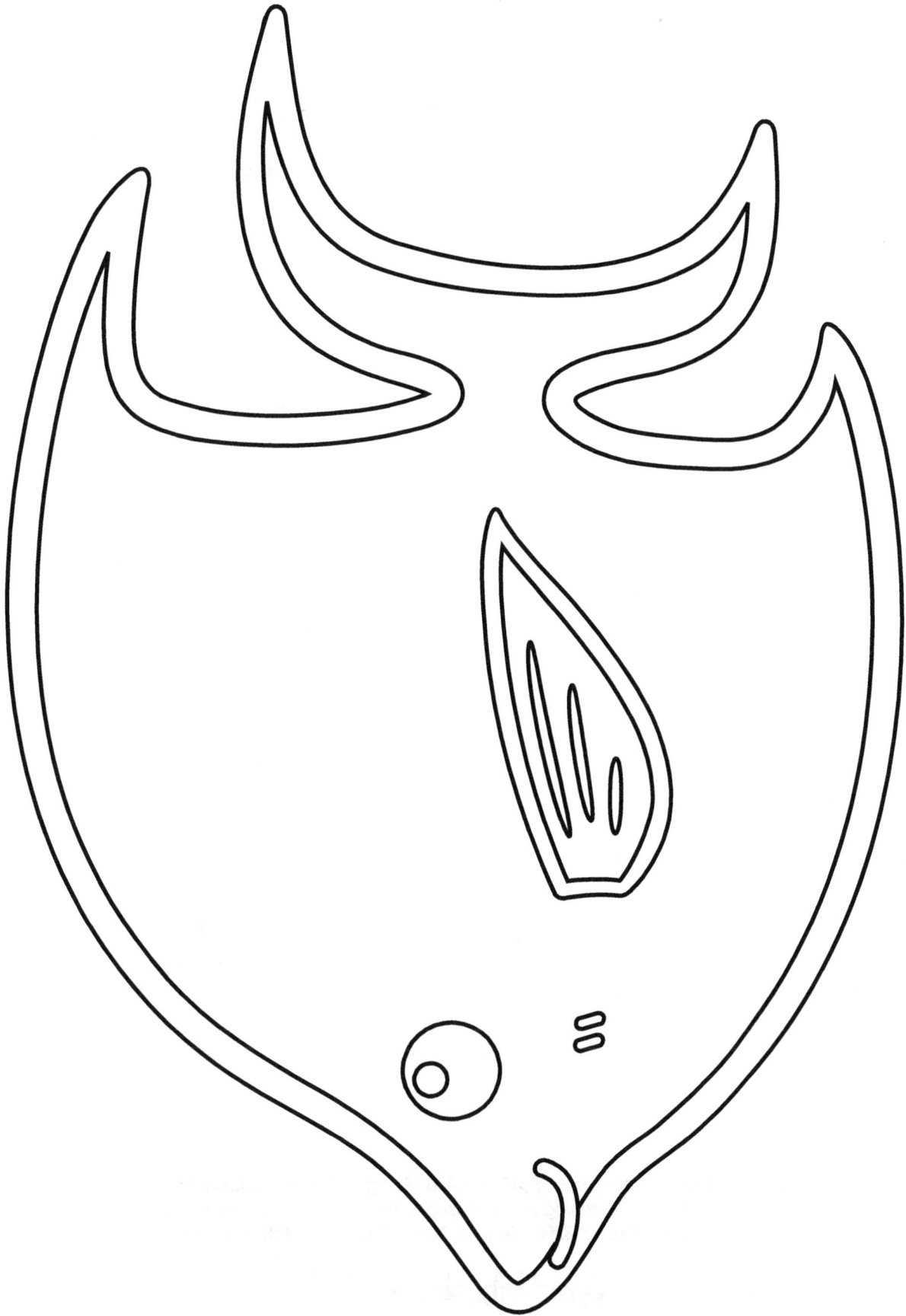

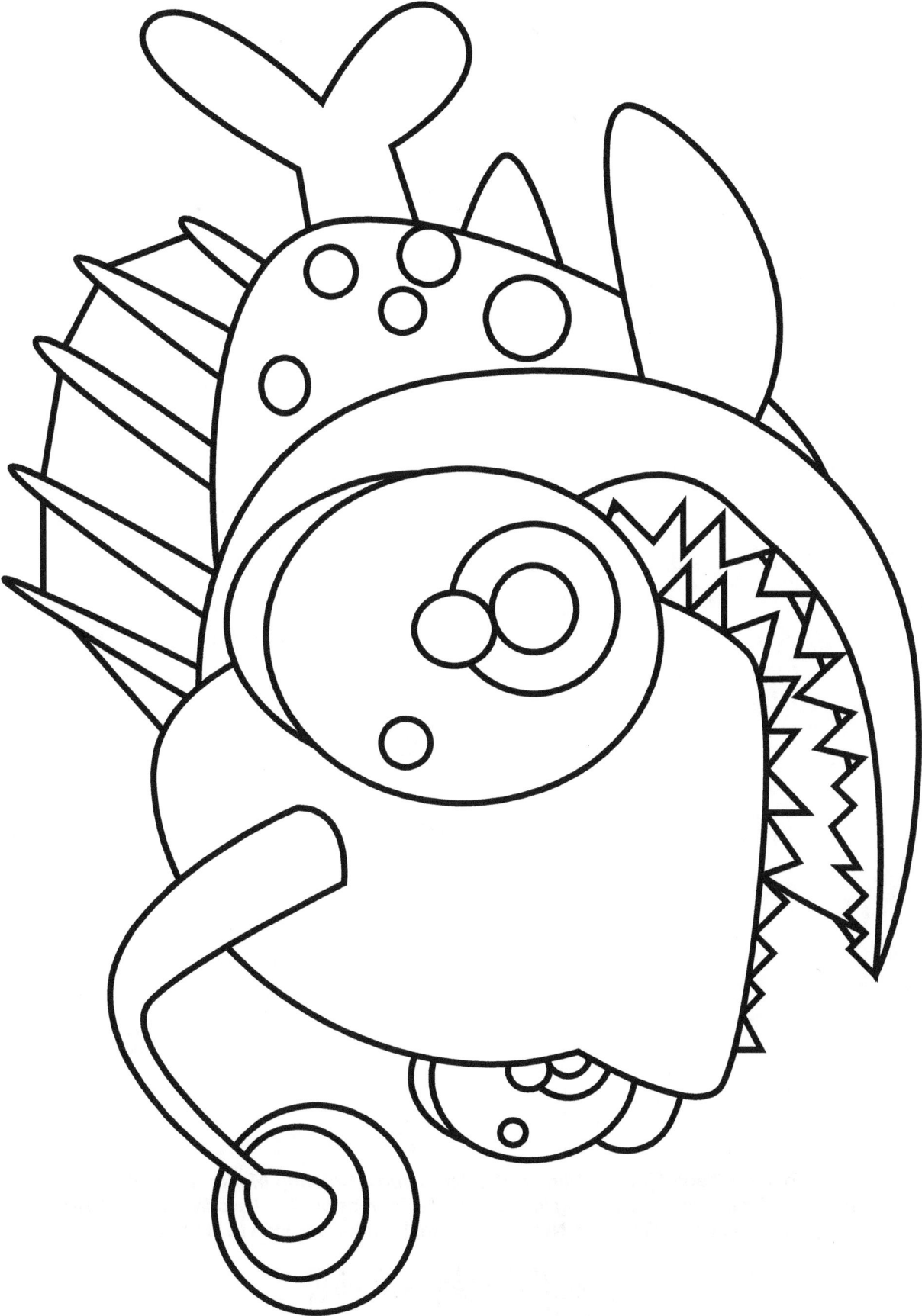

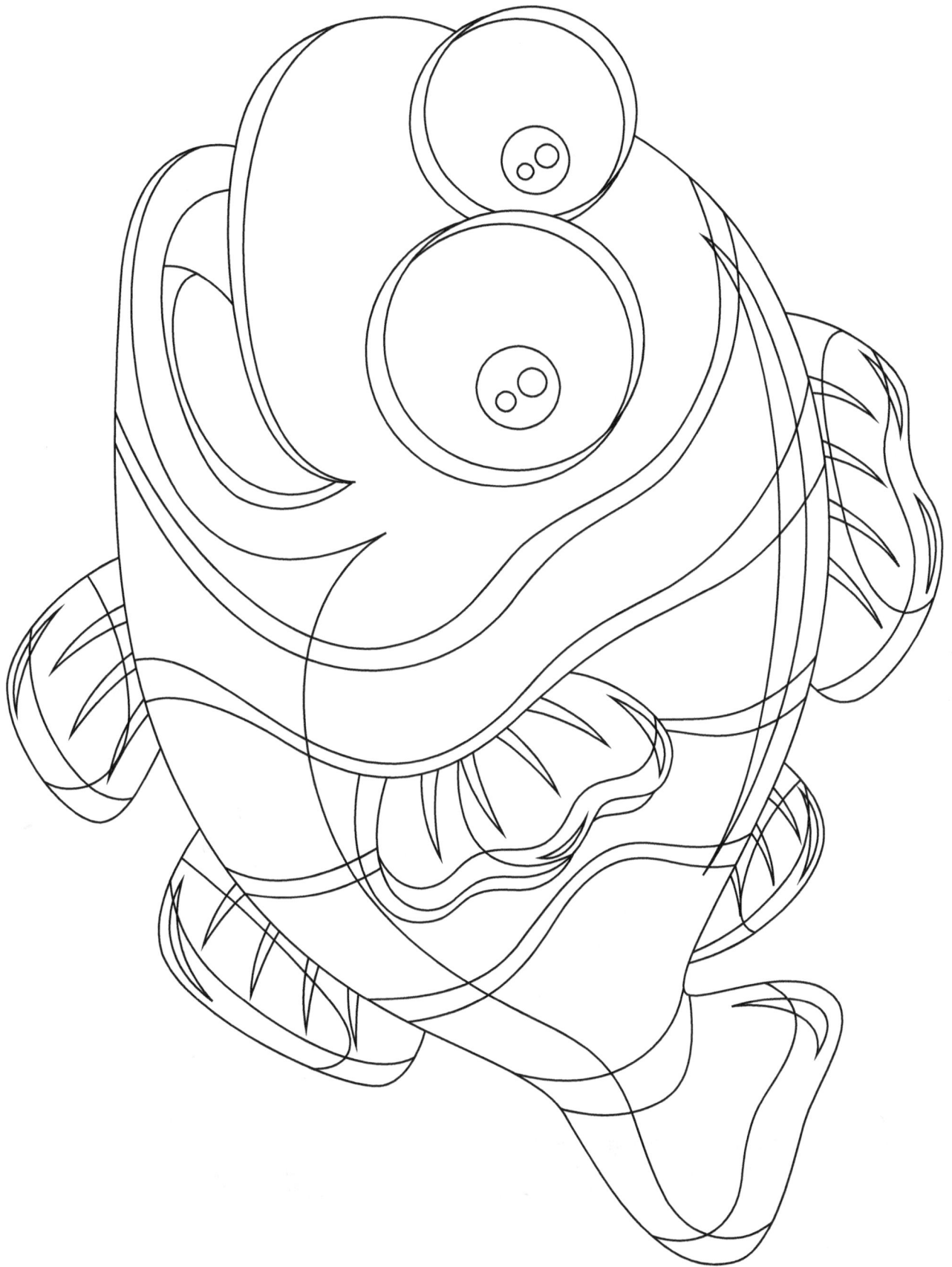

www.ingramcontent.com/pod-product-compliance
Lightning Source LLC
Chambersburg PA
CBHW081339090426
42737CB00017B/3206